Tales
of a
Valiant Soldier

Cameron McKnight

ISBN: 9798448004407

CONTENTS

Tales of a Valiant Soldier

ACKNOWLEDGMENTS

To my future offspring and whom it may concern…

TO MY FUTURE OFFSPRING

I pray that Heaven
Or wherever your spirit is initially manifested
Instills in you innate abundance
Appreciation
Sincerity
Integrity
And purpose…
I pray that you beseech God and find your foundation early on
In this life full of continuing social norms
I pray that your focus is unwavering
In the midst of all of life's trials and successes
Thereby granting you victory over the hidden serpents
Of which, can only be deduced or detected
With clear thought and rationale
I pray that you know and love yourself first
Show yourself how to love you
Before you attempt the rationality of loving someone else
I pray that although you may get weary on your journey
You know how to stand
Stand for your morals and convictions
Stand even when you've been knocked down
Stand against evil
And dare to be an even greater man
For your legacy is truly more about who you were and what you did
For others
Rather than what you amassed during your time of physically being

I pray that you know enlightenment
By this I mean, a glowing cadence of which your smile lights up the room
A sequential modulation that knows when to glow and when to be still
Thereby granting you victory over life's stills

I pray that you surround yourself with those of whom you consider to be
Great
No matter their circumstances
To uplift you during a woe
To motivate you to continue to go
To propel you to showcase your glow

For there will be those who try to hinder who you are —
Especially when you're unlike the rest
But to be you, who you are, early on

Is to be truly triumphant and unique in your younger years

I pray that you don't let any generational curse hinder you
You are you, even if you are part of me
And let no one tell you otherwise
I pray that your spirit is warm
I pray that your ideals are justified
And I pray that you know,
Whether I'm physically or spiritually there,
I'm always close by if you need me...

For your generation's lifetime, I can only theorize the wonders of
Advancements
And technologies
Those of which, I can only predict
But I can legitimately imbue in you
The justifications of my experiences
So that you're well equipped...
Society told me how to feel about these things
Nowadays, in my era, you hear so much repetition with how you should be
I'm living in a time where we are normalizing disfunction
So hopefully with the way I've arranged these words with my experiences,
Will make you ultimately see that you must...
Smile
Laugh
Have fun
Cry
Work hard
Stumble
Get up
Crawl
Fuss
Walk
Scream
Run
Dance
Fly
Take a risk

Yours truly,
Cam

WHERE DID WE LEAVE OFF?

Ah yes, the foundation
The foundation as the most pivotal part of one's being
Signifying how they'll operate, respond, grow, and ultimately fall
Throughout the course of their lives
I remember writing about this when I was younger
And yet...
So many experiences I had not yet had
So many encounters I had not yet come across
So many ideas that had not yet provoked my mind
But this ideology that I came up with in my younger days
Was vital to my overall development as a young man

To stay my course
To ensure my growth
To respect not only myself but others

But all of this sounds fair and good
When it wasn't all fair and good
For life has a way of testing you with its trials and tribulations

So what happened after I wrote about this ideology?

Well to that question, here are some of my journals

Beginning immediately after GENU was completed...

1. I'M A THINKER

At all times, I must think about what comes next
I can't live in the moment
I can't be out here living reckless, for I believe my soul is too precious
I must abide by my morals, standards, and convictions
With the upmost resolve
Therefore I can always claim victory in the overall war
Even if I lose a few battles…

I wonder what's coming next?
I know we're on the cusp of some major advancements and bullish runs
Especially with the fall of the economy that recently happened
Everyone should know now is the time to make those investments
Not just financially but in themselves
Although I'm not able to do much now,
I believe I've made some investments that will secure my freedom in
Chapter 1 of my life…

I wonder why I don't "reach" many people?
Not many people actually sit down and have a deep conversation with me
I believe I give off an image that's not my image
Maybe I should be more in cahoots with my true image?
Because alienation is what I've always felt aligned to
Thus, I jest at the fact that I'm seen as being popular
Thoughts that plague my mind…
I'm trying to be the best younger version of me but I see myself failing
And I can't grasp ahold of my failures and turn them around

You know what?
It's really scary to be in your thoughts
And to believe that you're failing yourself, simultaneously…
When externally, it seems like you're winning!
Hmm, such a monstrosity!

I'll end this here, as it's turned into a ramble
And I know that It'll all work out!
I know me and I know what I am capable of
So many say I'm still finding it, because I'm so young
But they haven't had a genuine conversation with me
I know where I'm at in life now
And I know where I want to be
I got this!

2. ME VS. ME

The realization of my born into situation,
Is a perplexing vex that significantly impacts gestures
And looks towards me…

Although I am a thinker
I know where I was born
I know how I portray myself
And I know that I'm still learning

And the biggest battle that I will face in this life
Is not with any of life's temptations, seductions, or vices…
But it will be with myself
It'll be Me vs. Me
For I will only be as good as I allow myself to be

Cause I remember…
I remember how I've had to grow up
I remember the longing I've felt
I remember the times where I ain't have

And with all of these memories in tact, I just want to break the cycle
I have to do this for not only myself, but for who's coming after me

Become the real Cam
Showcase the real Cam
Love the real Cam
And embrace the real Cam as a man

Teach myself those lessons that I haven't been taught
I will do this!
I've already laid the foundation

I spent all those nights learning
I'm in high school, but I've spent all those nights learning
And still do!
I can't even voice everything to everyone…
I believe in 4 things right now
God
Myself
Cybersecurity
And cryptocurrency

I understand that taking the path as I currently am,
Will potentially lead to a toxic obsession
But I must do this to have it early
As long as I stay in cahoots with my morals
And never blame my adolescence for getting out-of-tone
I believe I can go through this phase of "toxic obsession"
And come out unscathed

But I wonder how many people I will hurt on the way?

I can't help the innate looks
I know there will be hostile crooks
I know that this path will not allow me to "fit in"
But I know that I'll meet some gentle souls in the end
Who will see through it all…

3. THE SNOWFALL DIDN'T FALL THAT WINTER

It's been a tough year
I've been trying to deduce and reason the origination of the phrase
"Diamond in the rough"
To identify those things and people
Who I believe bring great value to the world
I want to understand more
I want to propel myself further
With intense fervor, I aim to grow and learn to be a herder
Not a usurper, but a person who brings forth the light
That people are willing to believe in

Like the people I've looked up to until now
From Fred Rogers to Howard Hughes
Those are lights, for disparate reasons,
That I could only dream of manifesting

But one day…
One day I say
Things will start going better for me
I've laid the foundation
I've made the investments for my structure
I'm just currently standing out here on faith for my time to come

For I will be heard!
People will have begin to have deep conversations with me
Rather than having superficial (surface level) ones because of my age
I will one day show my offspring something different
Than what I went through (and currently going through)
I will become smarter
I will help those in need
All while making my one dream come true!

I just have to stay true
With all the temptations and distractions that have yet to come
I have to remain vigilant

To overcome those serpents
As you can't leave your grass cut too high
Because snakes can hide and lurk in the grass

Maybe I'm just spouting all of my ideals

Because I'm struggling with something...
I feel like I'm looking for something to "wake me up"
I know what it's like to be alone
I deal with it a continuous basis
And studying is one of my outlets
Amongst other things
But I have definitely been searching for something...

But on another note...
I just now peeped out the window
And realized there was no snow
The holidays are upon us now
But I feel nothing
No holiday spirit
No nothing...

4. MAYBE I SHOULD LAY IT ALL OUT

The theories
The vision
The vices
The mission
The dream
The preclusion…
All constantly engulf my mind

I must say they have been for quite some time
But I've been pondering on the time where I'll be who and where
I want to be

I've always told myself to simply voice me
But I can't find myself being me right now
As I've said before…
There's definitely something hindering me

Maybe I'm terrified of failure
Maybe I'm worried about expectations
Maybe I'm anxious about the future
Even though I know what I must do…
What a line to be able to say in high school
But it still sounds of one who is a genuine fool

I say a genuine fool because it sounds as the following:
I'm terrified of failure
Because I'm scared to see someone better who succeeds at what I fail at…
Therefore I must have a slight ego
I am worried about expectations
Because I operate on the fixation of people's approval…
Therefore I must not be fully confident in myself
To potentially fall and get back up even better and/or stronger
I am anxious about the future
Because I want to be able to plan for all things accordingly…
Therefore I must be a slightly mad

Or maybe I'm thinking through everything too much
Maybe I'm just completely wrong and off
I'm writing too many "maybes"
I try to do self reflections of myself
But then I come back with more questions and sporadic thoughts

I guess the best way for me is to talk about it all
What I feel
How I should heal
What I plan to do
The brevity of my existence
What drives me
What provokes me
Etcetera
It starts here…

I'm Cam
I have a dream
That dream has been in my mind ever since I was a kid
I have goals that I want to achieve
On the pathway to realizing my dream
I want to be steadfast in my endeavors
Leading humanity down a path without terror
I want to be curiously passionate
About what will provide for the future of mankind
And for my kid(s) and/or successor(s) coming after me
I want to be capable of being multi-faceted
I want to look back
When I die
With my Creator, at my entire life
And never turn away
I want to be brilliant
Not just like Galileo, Da Vinci, Einstein, etc
But I want to be someone that those behind me and way ahead of me
Look up to
Even if I'm not the smartest
Even if I'm not the wisest
For I know I'm not the greatest
Even though I aspire to be…
I just want to clear a new path
One that's different than the social norms
That I'm accustom to hearing of
And witnessing…
I don't and won't always follow the rules
But I definitively believe in moral compass
If I don't follow the traditional rules of success
Then I could potentially inspire so many generations coming after me
To genuinely….
Take a moment and think

Think on what to do in this life
Think on how to be in this life
Think early on
In your adolescence
To maneuver (chart) this jungle in your younger adult years
And to be a game changer
For a game changer doesn't have to be rich
A game changer doesn't have to have the most influence
But when a game changer walks into the room
People know it,
Or at least that's what I currently believe

I still have so much to learn
I mean as I'm reading over this journal entry
I could potentially be speaking out-of-turn
But I must spell it all out in writing
For I know I have to go through some major trials and tribulations
Heck, I've even said that I don't believe
I'm adequately prepared for all of what's coming to me
Even though I've made a tangible game plan
But I will still stand

I write to myself right now
Feeling like a polymorphing Janus particle in a ferrofluid maze enclosure
Toxicity low
But irritation high
Every time I try to find my way out of the maze
And chart this new path that I speak of,
The ferrofluid maze enclosure changes
Creating a new final pathway to get out of it
All while I continuously morph into different forms
Learning constantly
And never settling for one form
And this is way beyond the norm
That I hear so many people causally speak of
Especially in your adolescent years…
But when I finally reach the end of the ferrofluid maze
If I ever do
Since it's ever-changing
I genuinely wonder who I'll be…

But I'm going to calm down now
For when my offspring read this decades down the line

I wonder what they'll think…
I write about these things so that if I'm not around
Or if they can't relate to me
Then they understand where my mind was at
During that stage of my life

I not only want to give them something I've never had
But I want my legacy to be profound

I know I have some demons that I have to address
But hey, isn't life truly a test?

5. THAT OLE' WATER TOWER

I decided to climb up today
So I could get away
Second to last journal entry I had to spell it all out
And as I always say
Relaying a visual
Will entertain the physical
And that will become something that's livable
But I climbed up today to reflect once again on
What I'm doing right now
How I'm acting right now
And am I learning the right things outside of high school right now
But to my shock there was another attendee
Every time I've come here
I've been alone intentionally
But there was a kindred spirit who saw me climbing
Seemingly curious
They yelled, "Why are you climbing?"
Not knowing my name
And me not knowing them
I exclaimed "To get away"
I didn't understand why they were here
But I genuinely felt no fear
My quick assumption was to think they had a "getaway" near mine
So they willfully invited themselves up
Even though I was reluctant
We introduced ourselves and there was a lot of upfront trust
I say that due to the discussions that we had
The discussions of the future and past
As it pertains to water, the economy, the environment, cryptocurrency,
And the Council of Nicaea to name a few
I was legitimately shooketh…
As I had NEVER come across someone who was as knowledgeable
And interested in such things
Being the same age as I
It's unheard of…
I got excited and yet they were calm
So I had to ask, "How are you so calm?"
They replied saying, "I believe in destiny…
Therefore we were destined to meet.
I had a feeling I would meet someone who was pretty cool soon."
I said, "Why?"

They said,
"Because when you're going through the cataclysm of harsh times,
Expect something refreshing soon"
I took note of that
And we both laughed
A few more conversations stewed
And then they said that they'd bid me goodnight soon
But before that
They had one more question
And that question was, "Why are you, you?"
I took that question meaning, "Why and how am I the way I am?"
And from there a more personal conversation brewed
I answered and then asked about the "cataclysm of harsh times"
They initially replied by giving me the eye
An eye so striking, yet intent on its gaze
It left me without any words to say
That's the first time I've witnessed someone look into my soul
And "still me"
"Still me" with no words
"Still me" with no facial expressions
But I knew I had to show willing intent
Therefore I never lost eye contact
And once they realized that I was serious
And that they could no longer pretend to forget that I had asked
They responded with, "Based on our conversations of it all,
I believe you know of them too…"
I didn't respond
They smiled, started to leave and said "I'll add you to my prayers"
I said "Why?"
And they said, "In that case, I'll pray for you even harder"
Then they left, while I stayed
And I wondered to myself, "How can you really meet a person like that, in a day?"

Now I sit alone on the tower in my normal silence
I'm thinking about the whole day
And what just transpired
Word for word
Topic for topic
It's now getting dark out
And the wind has started to pick up
I'm about to head on home
As I write this entry
But I hope I get to see the Attendee again soon

Sooner rather than later…
My getaway spot never fails me

6. THE ATTENDEE AND I

A few months have passed
The Attendee and I have kept touch
We work on STEM-related projects together
Together, we've created some incredible designs
Researched some new (baselines) avenues to make our planet Earth
More sustainable
And even explored futuristic conceptions that will define our lifetimes
The Attendee is extremely capable
Even I find myself sometimes marveling at their raw brain power
And this marveling has made me become even more committed
Committed to learning
Committed to growing
Committed to elevating above what I was born into
And my initial thoughts of what I thought that I could achieve
I'm starting to see, that the people you surround yourself with
Can truly make all the difference

As of right now, I don't feel like something is "hindering me" anymore
I don't feel an opposite force
I don't sense "the shadow"
I feel refreshed, I feel relieved
Which is a crazy feeling for me
As we don't only tackle STEM related things
But we have meaningful, deep conversations

Just the other day,
We discussed John Denver, John Krakauer, and Christopher McCandless
A type of lifestyle that we want to incorporate into affordable,
Environmentally conscious, prefab homes for the general populous

We've discussed that our generation is on the brink of change
A change in computing, finances, environmental conscious, real estate,
And the decentralization of things (the DoT we call it)
All of these changes are going to come about in the next decade
And we feel ready
With what little money we have
We've made the investments
With our smarts
We've made the plans

I mean heck, we're even aiming to go to the same college together
And we will succeed
We're dreaming
Daydreaming at times
Yet we're making progress

We've entered into a few competitions here and there
Won a few even
And I'm just having so much fun
I truly am
Even in my situation
I find myself smiling more
And when I find myself nearing peak capacity
I get inspired by dwelling in a realm that I formerly knew nothing of
And my capacity increases exponentially
It's such a deliberate, beautiful vicious cycle
Of which I'm enthralled to be in its grace

So many topics
So many thoughts I have to say
But I'm in a happy place right now
A happier place than I've ever been
And I can't wait to look towards the future

7 DON'T FLY FROM ME

Even though Heaven is so far away...
I wish that Heaven would let me through...
Because our world was robbed today
I know for a fact that the Attendee
Never thought that God would call so early
Especially with how the unfortunate events played out
For the Attendee and I will no longer have..
Anymore days of intriguing topics of conversation
Anymore days of random songs,
That I come to love,
That I would never find by myself...
Anymore days of STEM competitions and collaborations in the notebook
Anymore days of expressing the pressure of our born into situations
Anymore days of dreaming and fixating our sights on what's to come
Anymore days of exciting, exhilarating, random experiences
That are beyond the traditional of teenage years

I could continue on
But I won't blabber on
For it's sad that the world will never know just how powerful you were
The impact that you had on myself
The impact that you had on your family
And the impact that you had always said you wanted to have
On the universe
As I've said before, it was truly marvel-worthy to watch your brain go
And the world will never know such the scale of tragedy
That occurred today...

I find myself festering up an angry sadness, yet I show no emotion...
Like an amulet attached to me,
Holding back everything that is swelling from within
The Attendee's parents called me to check-in
And on the phone I could only blame myself
So selfishly...
Blame myself for not being there to change events
Of which I have no control/authority over
For the Attendee knew how much of a strain I put on myself to be me
But seemingly, God had another plan
But I wonder how taking away someone so potentially vital
To humanity's progress and loved ones
And of whom, played a significant role in my life,

Is the correct plan?
It makes me wonder,
"How much suffering I will have to go through in my life?"
Because the way I see it,
If I'm going through all of this and more so early on,
I'm going to have to go through some major strifes in this life

There was one conversation I recall having with the Attendee
It was on the topic of,
"How to deal with moral convictions in modern society?"
The Attendee and I came up with the same conclusion of,
"Genuine moral convictions, amongst the younger generations,
Typically make one unpopular"
And thinking on that more,
I hope in the face of this tragedy, that I can remain valiant
I'm still on the younger end of the spectrum, and although I innately think,
I don't want to fall into a void based on my current erratic emotions

I locked away the notebook that houses all of the designs,
Thoughts,
And schematics
Made by the Attendee and I
There were two keys to open it
One key, I left at water tower
The place where the Attendee saw me first.
For time to degrade and erode it for the decades to come
And remember our presence
The other, I threw in the lake
The place where we always became relieved by looking at what was beyond
The lake itself

Although I'm still in high school,
For the first time in my life, I'm genuinely hurt
And I wonder how I will actually respond

For I hope your soul continues to dream
And you're granted the lab you always wanted
I hope God doesn't tell you all of the answers
Before we have the satisfaction of solving them
Take care

8. I FOUND MYSELF DANCING WITH YOUR GHOST LAST NIGHT

I remember all of the times in life that we cherished
Working hard and loving it harder
To one day be united in a lab with extreme ardor
And it bothers me
That you are no longer a sight I see
Just a representational apparition of what I had profoundly wished to see
Be?
Were we to be or not to be?
I'm dastardly stricken by the solitude of mind's debris
Constantly plaguing me with the aches and thoughts
That sporadically remind me of we
Together
Knotted
Strong-hearted...
But last night
You and I were supposed to be allotted...
Allotted an audience by the Father's charges
And this audience should have foretold to time itself
To disregard the sanctions of the space-time
For we would've been together on His time
I'm talking more than just visiting hours
I didn't want a repetition of scheduled appointments
I wanted an audience of which I could ask Him
If I could take you Home
To your mother
To your father
To your siblings
Maybe then what we aimed to become
Could've been manifested even through the tragedy
But we weren't allowed this audience...

So I took the dance last night to relive the moments
Ponder and dream on the times that bestowment was almost upon us
And apparently, in that moment, I could feel what was real
The smile
The laugh
The ghost
The fervor
But it didn't help me heal

Only ensure my zeal for overcoming the long suffering...
And just like that, after the dance, I woke up
As a pair of wild quail flew beyond my window
What does that symbolize?
For I'm not the wisest
But I know that implies the allies
Meaning, where one goes
The other go
A joint account that melodizes
In the circumvention that bonds these birds together
Whether or not, I will see you again is a question that I must deduce myself
But if God so happens to grant us both those spiritual wings
Heavens gates shall open for us to fly into ourselves...
Maybe then we'll accomplish the theories that we spoke about
Laugh again about the unknown trajectories
Of which we planned refined routes...
And to that I'm excited...
I used to say
I'm Fred Rogers
You're Howard Hughes
And to that you were always amused
But I remember what goals you aimed to achieve in this life
Your family said that you had talked about them your entire life
And although your physical is gone
Your soul still lives on
Manifesting a voice
That gives me suggestions on my movements
I just hope that the voice lasts long...

The two goals that you wanted to achieve
I don't have the particular mind to heed
But I told your family that they will not need
Meaning, one day
I'll take care of school for two of your family's generations
To one day hope that a mind like yours comes about
And steers society in the right direction
I am the social reject
You were the calming yet burning intellect
No one can replace that
And the dance that I took last night
Until the day, we're in the Heaven's lab working tirelessly again...
Reminded me that
You were genuinely, my friend

9. HOW COULD THIS HAPPEN?

Everything worthwhile
In these younger years of mine
Feels as though it's been taken from me
My genuine friend
My blessing
My health
And now my best friend

You told me on our final haircut together
That you wouldn't see me graduate
Nor would you see what I accomplish in this life
But I wasn't prepared for it to actually happen…

I feel as though I've fallen for a lie
Like all the odds will forever be stacked up against me
And never be with me
Last night I asked God what I did to have all of this happen…
I find myself getting more and more intertwined with the causality of man
And I feel like I'm becoming a monster…
A robotic monster of sorts to better describe it
I don't sleep much anymore
I'm restless
I spend practically all my free time in books
That'll advance my well-being for the future
And I'm neglecting everything else
Even though I'm trying to remain "hang worthy"
As a robotic monster, I'm letting my knowledge scream
For I know not what else to do…
I'm clueless
Currently in a state that I know I must overcome soon
To ensure myself as myself
Such a dire situation
But I'm back on my former toxic nature
Trying to become abundantly astute in all areas of interest
And personally deemed relevance
Throughout the tireless pursuit
I'm learning more about Pontí
And intertwining his works with Gresham's Law
I'm learning more expert topics of computer science and its by-laws
I'm dwelling in the realms of cybersecurity and cryptocurrency again
Because that will be the immediate future in the coming years

But I still have quite the love for astronomy and physics

These days,
In my current life,
I'm supposed to be planning for my next steps after high school
I know not what to currently choose
But knowledge will be my fuel
I'm at a loss because I haven't had the time to sit down
And deal
And heal
From all of what's occurred
And since I'm not able to do that
I'm going to go full-speed-ahead even more so
And hope for the best...
I'm at a time of unease

God, be careful with my heart

10. THE DECLINE BITTERNESS

Did you know that one of the greatest sins is to destroy and betray yourself
For nothing?
Yet so many people do it on a day-to-day basis
Even when the odds and life is in their favor
They somehow manage to do the unthinkable, continuously
When they don't have to go that route
When they have people in their corner
When they have viable options of sustainability
And yet…
They continue

I don't categorize myself as any different
Because I feel the bitterness seething more and more from me
I realize and acknowledge all of the blessings and bestowments
I've been given…
And to that I am truly grateful
But I feel the hurt
Yet it doesn't show
As I said in a prior journal, I've been asking God, "Why?"
More and more
As cliché as it sounds
I believe, the saving grace of my fate will be to experience
I was brought up with my circumstances
In a relatively small town, and my experience currently doesn't reach far
I'm a man who's interested in knowledge
And as I am now restless these days,
I pursue it more and more
I desire to learn about more religions
To better understand how people think
I desire to learn more about cultures
To sincerely appreciate and admire the variety of mankind
As there are many tribes I'd like to make contact with
I desire to learn more about the way the world works
From financials, to laws, to the intricacies of business, to the accountable
STEM topics
Of which I have not yet all dwelled
But in contradiction,
I have no desire for anything that is upcoming in my college years
I need not to find myself
I only need to become it
By dwelling in the realms of more complex technical topics,

College may have a genuine impact
But the way the education system is setup
I have doubts I'll be learning what's essential
Until I hypothetically enter a post-graduate program
Or put my foot down when I initially enroll,
And continue to conduct high value self-study
As I've done in my high school years

But I'm declining
Already…
The man who I wanted to be at this age,
The last winter before college
Is not here
But what is here
Is a boy
A boy who's failed so many times
A boy who's searching for something
A boy who's ego is overbearing for his own self
A boy who has not forgiven himself for being no more than a human
A boy who is simply not good enough
And although he realizes it, his pride will not let him say it
I didn't realize the effect that my upbringing,
Would have on me at this stage in my life
I know exactly what I need to do
And I'm not able to do it

Knowledge can open doors
Motivation can knock doors down
Egos can close doors
And bitterness,
For whatever personal reason it may be,
Can burn the building to the ground

I need to be more in cahoots with myself and act on it accordingly
I am not,
And will never be,
At the point where I will let the vices of life
Overtake my conviction and morals
But I must get ahold of me to truly become great

I must stop questioning God and seek the answers that I inquire
All while trusting Him at the same time

I will not let this bitterness

This anger manifestation
Overpower me
I'm still Cam

But I must go on a few trips
To get the grip I need on myself
That will eclipse these strongholds
My insouciance
Will eventually overpower these strifes
With the knowledge I have yet to gain
A melange of the sporadic thoughts,
Knowledge,
Vices,
Powers,
And capabilities
That are not estranged from me being me

Yet I must adhere and admit to currently being amaroidal

11. I HAD NO TIME TO CHOOSE

It's that time now
It's now spring
It's time to make a decision on my future
It's time to dictate what and who I will become based off one decision...
Wrong!
The choices and investments I made in myself during these years
Will pay exponentially more than what college will do for me
I truly believe that

All of the untold hours learning to program/code in a variety of languages
All of the untold hours learning finances
All of the untold hours contributing to the blockchain
All of the untold hours competing in cybersecurity competitions
What a ride it has been
I wish the Attendee was still here
What a celebration of feats it would be
But I try not to dwell on that these days

I've found some new acquaintances
Who are all likeminded individuals
We share all types of ideas and plans we have
We discuss personal topics
We even plan to work together on multiple initiatives and ventures
All-throughout college
We have not yet talked about our adult lives
I hope they will become my genuine friends
But I know not where to go school
And I have no time to choose

Although wanted,
I'm walking aimlessly in rectangular prism chamber with black hole doors
All-around
Because I'm young,
Even though somewhat knowledgeable,
The only way I can make this decision make sense for me
Is to play it safe
Even though I know it's not the optimal decision
Based on my presented opportunities...

So I'm going to play the game of "standard life rules"
And also make a huge investment in myself before I enroll

To ensure that if things go bad
I'll have something to fall back on

I'm not in the mood for what this next chapter will bring

I'm in the mood for the experiences
That most people never get to have in life
Of which have the capability to mold me
Mold me into what I consider to be my ultimate form

I'm still finding myself in a bad place mentally
And I also find myself blaming my adolescence more these days
Instead of fixing what I know needs to be fixed
It's almost as if I'm intentionally trying to regress myself
Like I've done for quite awhile

But enough blabber
I have no time to choose
And I'm not in the best mood
So I will play it safe

I truly wonder what sort of monster, beast, robot, etc
I will become in the years to come...

12. I HATE IT HERE

It's never quiet
The rustling and bustling of warm bodies
Ever massages my mind
I desire some peace
Some peace to appease the propensity of my innate existence
I'm not one for a fuss of any sort

I feel completely alone and ostracized
I'm not defined by the likes of the general populous
Therefore I'm crucified
Whether it's by my own doing
Or the doing of others
That is where I stand

I no longer want to trust God's plan
Instead I want to figure it out myself
This is something that only fools do
But I guess I'll be the fool
As I was born into a time where God is no longer feared
And I can see it here

Maybe I haven't given here enough time
But I believe that my vision is clear
In the realization
That I hate I here

13. IF ONLY YOU UNDERSTOOD

I'm beginning to once again realize that I still haven't come to terms
With everything that has occurred in my life
It's breaking me, slowly
And the environment I'm in
It's tearing me down
And no one has realized it

But one day I know it'll cause a huge breakdown
Because I'll continue to repress it all until it explodes
Or implodes (all the same)
Such foolishness I speak
Yet I continue heed

I want to harp on something that I just wrote…
"No one has realized"
I'm literally an outcast …
I'm ostracized
I'm crucified for being me
I'm terrified
I've developed traits that aren't glorious
Glorious in the sight of a Creator
Nor myself
And I try to blame it on circumstance
When did I ever become a man who blames?!
When I was younger, I was more of a driving force
Than I am now…

1 Peter 3:14 reads, "But and if ye suffer for righteousness sake, happy are
Ye: and be not afraid of their terror, neither be troubled"

I need to get back to this thinking
And not let my surroundings
Change the view
Change the vision
Change me
Even if, I'm continuously questioning…

I just feel like I have no one, ya know?
I know all of these "fancy" words
Themes
Theorems

And theories
I've taught myself how to be multi-faceted
In an abundance of areas
I've contributed to something that will manifest greatly in the years to come

But what good is it all, if no one understands me
For me to showcase my prowess with my goals
And ultimately my dream
I have to be able to connect with people...

Am I just unlovable?
Has my toxic obsession with becoming great,
In all aspects of myself,
ruined me?
Did I not plan for something adequately?
I talked up all types of notions in my early years
But in the real world
They're crumbling
Not necessarily because of me
But because of the fact that I didn't account that the world was like this...

And to be alone in this world
Where no one can seemingly relate
Where no one can seemingly understand
Where no one can seemingly interpret
Is truly lonesome

I'm showcasing more of my human side
Rather than the robotic nature that people say encompasses me

I actually do feel...
Nor am I afraid to admit it
Physically
Mentally
And Emotionally
I, in fact, feel

I do desire an avid support system
I claim I don't
Cause I've made it here to this point
And where I'll eventually be
Primarily through my own grit
But that claim is still false

I must experience now more than ever
Because I'm at the stage where
I need to see it...
Before the full repression of everything explodes

I am told that I don't let people in
I am told that I'm too "tight-lipped"
I am told that my existence will always be that of a loner
They question my integrity
Without visibility of the tenacity that I showcase as an exemplary of my
Orderly rectitude
But who are they to tell me,
All of this,
When they have never spoken to me directly
I am, and always will, aspire to be the greatest that I can be

You see people love to talk through other people
And avoid direct confrontation
Why is that?

And when or if they finally do decide to confront one
It's out of one of the following:
Anger/Fear
Jealously
Animosity
Cowardice
Or mockery

People do not like what they can't fully understand
Even if they themselves, don't take the time to try to understand it

If my words and thoughts are telling me anything it's that...
Mental health is real
And it will become more and more of a factor in everyday life
For my generation and the generations after me
For we are a society who no longer fears anything greater than ourselves...

I'm going to go ahead and do what I must
To ensure that I can overcome
What I feel

And for me that is to explore the world
The cultures

The people
The lifestyles
The history
The purpose
All while cultivating and honing my skillsets

I'm going to do it before I implode…

11. MY SHORT TERM PLAN

Last few journal entries have been hard for me to write
As I haven't had a great time adjusting
To where I'm currently at
And my mental headspace has been lackluster …
But in these last few days, I've figured out something that I can do
I've found my skillsets to be in high demand
There are multiple opportunities for me to excel
And foster a creative, learning environment
Only if I am okay with stepping outside of my comfort zone
Let me explain…

I've been exuberant on the fact that
I don't have time for any of the college life
Thus, I have more free time
But I've formulated a plan
With these "new friends" that I spoke of
In my former journal entries
We're going to code/program new capabilities/tools almost every weekend
At different universities all across the USA!
It sounds absolutely splendid to me
Learning/honing skills in multiple programming languages
And sometimes proving the mathematics beforehand
All in one weekend
Against students from all over the globe!
Whew! I can't wait!

We've formed our team
And a schedule of how we will rotate members
Based on "usage", "location", "knowledge", "wins", etc.
And some other factors…
And can you believe it?
The universities all across the USA
Typically pay for the entire trip!

We have our first competition this upcoming weekend
Out in the Western part of the USA
Of which I've never been
So this will give me the opportunity
To meet new folks all over the USA
To experience more of what the world offers

And to put some more money in my pocket
Every
Single
Weekend!

My friends and I plan on doing this until we graduate
As we pass particular milestones that we've set for ourselves
Our resumés will be all-the-more stronger
And we will look for other opportunities to grow ourselves as individuals
As we succeed with this first venture
We've talked about buying tax deeds and liens
We've talked about a cryptocurrency investment management firm
We've talked about space mining
We've talked about new protocols of secure communication
We've even talked about prefab/modular units we could build
As a company and/or corporation!
One particular guy in this friend group
Has been teaching me the ins and outs
Of modern finances and taxes
But of course, I'm still conducting my own self-study
And in exchange
I've been teaching him all about the blockchain
From a hands-on, programming perspective

It is quite amazing to meet such like-minded people
Who are very similar in what they aspire to be
We haven't all grown closer yet
But we share goals
And we share likeminded outtakes on how to live life
I am hoping through these competitions that we can all grow closer

But tonight I'm getting ready for the competition this weekend
I know we will be victorious!

And as a side note
I think I've somehow failed a test here in college
But aced all the rest?
School seems like it'll be quite a chore
But I'm just not going to worry about that
Time to do the real studying on what matters for the future

Let's go!

15. MY EGO TOOK A HIT

I've come to realize
This world is full of talented people
Through these competitions
I've truly met some remarkable talent

And although we have won a few competitions
I recognize the capabilities of my peers
At some of these competitions...
These people are hungry
Whether they're morally sound
Doesn't matter in this case
But the gifts they showcase
Are truly magnificent

These experiences
Have been great for me
Not only for the technical capabilities
But because my ego has taken a much needed hit

I've learned more so what it means to be humbled
I realize what I'm capable of
And what I need to work on
I haven't given much thought to my mental state as of late
Due to being "in the zone" on these competitions
But maybe that's for the better?

I've sworn to myself to study everyday and get better
I've been neglecting all of my college studies
I feel like I'm back in high school
The dream that I have
And the goals I want to achieve
They've been so fun to chase
What a time!

16. I HAD AN EPIPHANY THAT DAY

Last night I had a memory
A memory of my grandfather
It was only he and I
We found ourselves at a well off person's home
My grandfather described he had never been in such an estate
And when we left and started driving back to our home
He said to me,
"All of that is something that I will never have in this life…"
I asked him whether or not he would want it if he was able to have it
He described that if he was at the place in life to have that type of choice
Then his resources would be allocated elsewhere in the intangibles of life
From that day forth, I knew I had to be able to have that freedom
To see my dream unfold

At this point and time in my life…
I've realized a couple things
And seen a couple things
I feel more inclined to showcase my true self
I feel more astute
Let me explain what I mean…

From the memory that I just recounted on
That has made the vision become more clear
I want to help people
I want to establish a humanitarian organization that can free people
Free them of their strongholds
Free them of their strifes
Free them of their born into situations

And then..
Create access to, what should be, legal human necessitates
Create access to significant opportunities
Create access to an abundance mindset

For a proper mindset is a powerful tool
And an abundance mindset is one that embraces, incorporates, and seizes
What others don't
And those are truly rare

During my travels, I've begun to surround myself in different cultures
And unique lifestyles

I've met some people who have made some everlasting impressions
On myself

I've began to realize the following…
I know I'm quite different than others in my field/area of expertise
And I know how important it is for me to truly be me
I have to leave a trail for those who come next
For those who right now don't see a way
And that is my overarching mission
Because I know that I'm capable

There are so many areas that I want to involve myself with
I want to help all things on Earth that require helping
I want to see our Creator's canvas blossom while I'm here
And when I'm gone

That means I have to hold myself to the highest standard of completeness
That is true to me
Otherwise I will fail

I know my time is coming for an implosion on everything I've built up
And not released
But I still
Right now
At this moment
Feel so pure
Ever free
And grateful

Peace is with me, momentarily
And I know what I have to do on this planet

The connections with people
The connections with what encompasses nature
The oceans
Other living organisms
And their futures
Are all too important
For me to forsake
When I have a goal

And I have like-minded individuals
In my corner
Who are are ready to become the leaders

Scientists
Pioneers
And Innovators
Of tomorrow

And that's what we have as human beings
The power to make the incredible happen
And I'm finally witnessing it
As I used to hope for

17. YOU HAVE TO BE STRONG

So many things in this life can hurt
And so many pertinent traits you must have in order to continue to stand
In the midst of what stands against you

As I've said before
My biggest battle has been me vs me
So I've studied myself silly
So I've begun to venture out to other sectors besides my area of expertise
So I've begun to travel all over to engulf myself in what life is on Earth
And I'm only a college kid…

My friends and I,
Ever since starting this initiative in tech competitions,
Have become closer
And I believe that we've become wiser
Not only in our technical specialties
But as human beings
They're all so formidable in their own rights and they push me to be better
As I do the same for them
We have even started a virtual weekly debate session
Where we play games like GloomHaven and Shogi
And discuss past, present, or future topics that we deem relevant
Not only in technology
Or finance
But in philosophy
History
And sociology
These topics are always debated in a respectful manner
Even if the debates become quite intense

Just the other day
My friend came to me to discuss the topic of societal medication
Medication in the sense of not being able to deal
With the common occurrences of life
And how the vast majority will look to some form of medication
To "not feel"
Whether that's drugs
Alcohol
Sex
Attention
Pornography

Substance abuse
And other rudimentary addictions

We discussed this in a manner from all aspects
That we felt inclined to stand from
As he and I grew up in different parts of the world
Under different circumstances
Because we both want to understand the viewpoints that make humans
Humans
So we discussed
And came to the following main idea that…
We are now living in a time where common societal norms
Aren't in the Creator's realm
And that will become more true as time continues
Until time itself resets

Thus the outcome of the conversation
Was simply,
 "You have to be strong enough to think for yourself,
The vices of life shall not be able to overtake you
If you have an unwavering conviction
And unyielding stance on what you believe to be true for yourself"

Religion typically tells us that through God or some form of a Creator,
It is easier to achieve this safe haven
By following their allotted guidebook/rulebook
And while that may be somewhat true
I beg to say that the most powerful humans in the world
No matter their status
No matter their monetary means
No matter their influence
Have achieved this through their own self-conviction of stance

You must be willing to think for yourself
No matter who teaches you or what you follow
Otherwise
You could find yourself blind to the whole world
And become a walking contradiction

For myself, I have started to see that my definitive truth
Is what I've believed since middle school
That I am nothing without fear of something greater than me
I am a human

I may be quite talented in some areas
But others are quite talented in the areas that I am not as strong
That's why I genuinely appreciate my friend group
Although I haven't made many connections
Here at my university
My friend group has done wonders for me
In the midst of my lurking shadows
For we are there to uplift each other
For we all know that we are a little unique and not the standard
For we want to be wise on life
And showcase our respective talents
For different dreams
But for common goals
And for that I truly thank them all

I have now started to become who I've always wanted to be
And I'm enjoying it
I've now studied plenty of religions
Engulfed myself in different cultures, music, and lifestyles
All while honing and curating my technical skills
In a more refined manner

The Attendee's words from back in the day were correct
"Cameron, to walk amongst the living as a duck, or a sheep, and not know
What is…
Is the highest form of pity one could embark on —
With the blessings we have as humans"

Which translates to,
"You must be strong and know of the meaning of abundance"

18. OUTSIDE THE BUBBLE

There is a war going on in Virunga…
Of which the privileged gloss over
The species
The landscapes
The economy
They're quivering
Quivering over unfortunate events
Yet they see no exact end

I've heard about potential solutions
I've read about actions being taken
I've seen the good-willed folks mean well
I've talked with those who want to see and be the change henceforth
And yet…
I've been saddened at the untimely losses of those willing to risk it all
For the legitimate cause

What must be done?
Most of those with privilege,
Like I
Only worry about making it big in society
By the following:
Having the homes
Having the cars
Having the career that leads to significant impact in that particular field
Having the amazing spouse
Having the beautiful children
Having the picturesque vacations
Having the multiple sources of income
Having the freedom to do what you like whenever you like
Ignorant to the reality that so many of our brothers and sisters
Deal with everyday

When did the "hustle" only become about getting rich and/or famous?

What is happening in this transformative society?
Of whom…
Puts the "riches" above morals
Puts the "sights" above conviction
Puts the "pleasures" above awareness

I understand that not everyone is going to,
Nor wants to,
Change the world
I understand that for some people,
They only care about changing the world for their family
I understand that for some people
The trials and tribulations,
Even in a privileged society,
Are hard enough to withstand
Especially when born under less than ideal circumstances
I truly understand all of this and more

But for me
And for my house
That stands on solid foundation
I must not bat-an-eye to the oppressions
Of privileged society and of developing society
Of those who look like me
And those who do not

For we are all native to one planet
Trying to figure out this thing called life

I must say that on my travels,
I've met some truly EXCEPTIONAL people
And these EXCEPTIONAL people have some of the greatest convictions,
Talents,
Ventures/efforts, etc.
That I could only gasp in awe at

But sometimes
Even these EXCEPTIONAL people are oppressed
Because…
For the church, they aren't holy enough
For the modern society, they have a limiting disability
For their loved ones, they don't look the same
It's madly saddening
Yet this is how everything has been since the dawn of humanity

From what's happening in Somalia,
Suriname,
Bhutan,
Armenia,
And many others

My diligence to stay relevant on matters of my personal
Deemed importance
Is in hopes to help, support, or learn from

As there are
So many cultures
So many perspectives
And so many experiences

For this is what I've been relentlessly searching for
Cause everyday we're alive,
We're granted with a chance
And a choice
My travels will continue until I cease
For my offspring will know and be made aware
Of genuine life
Outside the bubble

19. I WANT TO FEEL LIKE THIS

The human attachment of companionship
Is one that beseeches the hearts of many
Ever prominent with its precision
Ever abundant with its accuracy
Hoping to captivate
And enthrall the minds of its subjects
To the point of acting as a synthetic
Monoamine neurotransmitter
Causing so much good
In the right amount
Yet causing so much harm
If too sought after

Reflecting on this
I have never been a man of self satisfaction
Im not vulgar in any regard
I'm a refined
Well poised
Like a well-posed mathematical problem
Of this, I truly believe

But I feel as though I am now longing for companionship
After 20 or so long years
I am thinking about my legacy more so
Than I had ever before

My human side is coming out and the robot in me is cowering
Already...
I've travelled
I've discovered
I've engulfed
I've had major failures
I've had major successes
I've found out who I am
I've found out what I am
I've helped people worldwide
I've worked my butt off
I've witnessed...

And now I'm thinking about a team
A partner, potentially

Cause I wonder what it feels like...

I've felt unlovable for a long while
As I've described before in these journals
But now after I've done what I have
I am curious about the intrinsic human nature
That clings to genuine companionship
And affection
For I must believe that there is hope
In the unjust, unholy world that I live
Because hope without genuine belief is dead

Ahh, I must be genuinely losing my marbles...

20. CAN YOU SHARE THE THOUGHTS THAT YOU KEEP?

Today was a good day
But I'm coming to another realization..
And that is
It actually hurts to be left in the dark by the people you care most for

It's been a few years since the Attendee's death
But the Attendee's parents called me today
Inviting me to their summer family vacation
And their holiday gathering
They've stayed in constant contact with me
Ever since the beginning
And today, they mentioned once again
That I will always be their family
No matter how old
No matter what I do in life
I will always have a spot at their table
And their home
And if I ever need someone to talk to
They are just a call or text away…

You know, love is not hard
I don't believe in levels of love
But I do believe in different love types
Once you have genuine love for a certain person
There are certain things you just do naturally
Even if…
In spite of…
And no matter if…
This is something I can't be persuaded otherwise on
Because I've witnessed it firsthand

Genuine love
Doesn't fall victim to the ocular
It serenades in such the wonderful feelings
Of truly knowing
Of truly understanding
Of truly encompassing those intangible gifts
That the plaintiff so desperately seeks from a defendant

I know that I have been in the wrong sometimes

On how I've handled some situations
Because if I handle them appropriately
My feelings/emotions will reign over any practical reason
And that's part of why I know
That I'm very soon due to explode/implode

I feel it arousing in me
And I can't stop it
How silly am I based on these words I speak?
I guess I've partially fallen victim to what society says a man can "feel"…

I've studied so much
To see what ceiling I have
So I can go beyond it

I've engulfed myself in the cultures
To understand and gain new perspectives
So I can be a more well rounded individual

But I can't overtake,
Through brute force,
The part of me that makes me human

As I know from the people that I care for
Or have cared most for
I want complete honesty and straightforwardness

Just like those
Who cherish me,
Want from me

21. IT HURTS

It's holiday time
And I've consistently gotten bad news
From my health
To hearing about the untimely passings
Of some of my friend group

I feel like everything I've lived for
Was pointless
And that God has truly forsaken me and my friend's loved ones

The people who genuinely try to be different
The people who try to make a difference on this planet
Are met with so much misfortune and agony
While the others are seemingly met with so much glory
From any outside perspective…

Maybe God gives his toughest fights to his strongest soldiers…
But I've known so many wonderful people to fall victim to death
Untimely
By no fault of their own
And it hurts
It hurts so bad…
Because these are the people
Who would
And were,
Making all the difference on this planet
Without any wanted recognition
Without any significant monetary payment

It's hard to find real people
Like the people I've lost on this planet
They were truly marvel worthy…
And there will be:
No more nights of GloomHaven and Shogi
No more nights of enticing debates
No more nights of howling at the moon and stargazing
Through our custom-made telescopes
No more days of finding and fixing an ugly, old van
And traveling in it across the US until it breaks down
No more days of tech competitions across the US
No more days of flying in a scary mosquito helicopter

By a questionable pilot
No more days of new experiences hang gliding and paragliding,
And almost dying from them
No more days of thinking where we'll be when we're 25, 30, 40, 50, and 60

I'm hurt
And I'm just not okay

I feel like I need to quit everything
But I'll ensure,
What we all accomplished
In college years alone
And who you were as people
Are rightfully and justly exalted

Your loved ones will be taken care of forever
Even if the friend group,
Is broken forever as a whole

This is the worst holiday season I've ever had
And I'll miss you all greatly

God, you haven't been easy nor careful with my heart

22. THE CAUSALITY OF REPRESSION…
BREAKDOWN

I've quit everything
I'm questioning everything
I'm hurting everyday

But I will make it through
The people who I've helped all these years
Are right here
To help me

Cause I'm in bad shape
But I'll be back
And I'm thankful and grateful for all I have

My relationship with God
Will be better than ever

Before, I could quote an abundance of Bible verses
From the New Testament and the Old Testament
Like the pledge of allegiance
But after this event passes,
I'll be able to trust God through anything

You have to know how to keep the faith
And your sights on what you want to reach
Even in the midst of your struggles…

23. THE PEOPLE IN MY CORNER

One of the most important things in this life
Are the people you surround yourself with
If you find some trustworthy
Genuine folk
Who have dreams or goals like yourself
Keep them around

Some people will leave your life
Some people will even give up on you
But those who are meant to stay
Will stay
Quite literally
And quite simply…

The people on my team,
In my corner,
Have helped me in so many ways
To understanding personal and commercial real estate
To understanding finances
To understanding the intricacies of business
To being there to hear me out when I'm having issues
I'm so grateful and appreciative to them

In this most recent time
That I've been down
They've lifted me up
Quite literally…
And now as I stand firm again
I look to becoming all-the-more better
And doing even more in society

The goals that I've achieved thus far
Have been so fun to chase
And wouldn't have come to fruition
Without the folks who have genuine love for me

I remember when I used to write about not relating to people
And wanting that connection
But when I finally "extended" out
On my own accord
Although tough,

I found some good people for me

Not everyone is good for everybody
Even if they are an amazing person
Let me repeat that in another way...
You can meet a "perfect" person
And that not be who you need in your life

The beauty of humanity is in innate differences, ideas, and experiences
Justified reason doesn't account for free will and beliefs
That's part of what makes us, us
A mathematical chaos...

But my people
No matter where you end up
Will forever be my family
Thank you for helping me build myself back up

24. I ASKED FOR STRENGTH

I asked for strength
God gave me seemingly insurmountable difficulties

I asked for wisdom
God gave me problems to rigorously solve

I asked for courage
God gave me dangers to overcome

I asked for love
God gave me troubled people to sincerely help

I asked for victory
God had me fall down countless times so that I would know how to get
Back up stronger

I asked for motivation
God gave me experiences that he knew would push me to get out of bed
And work hard everyday

I asked for peace
God bestowed upon me a sincere calm in the face of my trials
And tribulations

I was never forsaken
I just went through some really tough times…
But now I'm here
And I'm able
I'm well-equipped

I have a dream
As outlandish as it is
It is my purpose

And the things that I plan to do
While working towards that dream

Well…
Let's just watch and see

The soldier in me, salutes the Heavenly Father

25. MET A KID YESTERDAY

I met a kid yesterday
He was just like me
Only better…
He was a light that lit up the room
Who's passion was marvel worthy
He talked about what he was gonna do on this planet
Yet he was only 4'2"

His mother told me how special he was
And everyone who came in contact with him
Agreed on the simple fact that he was different
In a profound way…

During my yearly holiday rounds
I just saw something in this kid, while I was walking through the halls

As he had so much pinpointed energy in making sure those around him
Were uplifted
Maybe I took interest because he also reminded me so much of myself
When I was younger

While speaking with him,
I looked in his eyes and thought of my future offspring
Whether they are adopted
Or my own seed
I could see my future offspring in front me
And I looked at his mother
And I broke down and cried
Apologizing and saying, "It's just not fair is it?"
She broke down with me
But the kid…
The kid was stronger than both of us
He said something along the lines of,
"Why cry when I currently have all the functions of life,
That other kids here would love to have, even for a split second…
So mister, don't get down on yourself, you being here is enough"
"And Mom, stop crying I want ice cream…"

I had been completely outclassed
And his mother knew it too

Life is so precious
Ask yourself, if what you're fretting over,
Is worth your unhappiness with the blessing you have of life
That others so desperately cling to or would like to have for a split-second

The kid has ignited another flame in me

26. YOU GOTTA BE

You can never quit
You can never surrender on your obstacle(s)
You must proceed
You must continue to fight...

You cannot make them love you
You cannot make them appreciate you

That's why genuine love
Should be treated with genuine care
Hold it close and hold it tight
The Fruits of the Spirit
And the Gifts of the Spirit
Will describe how it should be
But in reality
You know by unraveling the wrapper

You see...
All people on this planet
Have a wrapper
Unravel it until you know for yourself
Ask sincere questions
And find out what lies inside the wrapper

No strongholds
No strifes
No animosity
No prejudice
No discrimination
No hate

Say yes to spreading the love
Say yes to spreading the good news

Take note of who you tell good news to
And the relationship is never the same

Develop an abundance mindset
Develop a relationship with those
Who will give you their all...
Remember

A relationship isn't always romantic
Treasure those who are hard to find

Respect yourself
Know what you stand for early on
You're going to hear a lot about…
Standards
General populous activities
Disfunction normalization
And more

Be you
Don't conform
Don't be swayed on what you believe is right
Discover for yourself
Others,
Even if it's few,
Will come to those who they see are real

Be okay with being alone sometimes
This is one that you have to understand
As early as possible
Because if you don't…well…
I'll just continue on…

Be okay with making a sincere mistake
Or miscalculation
Don't fret too much
On being human
Know how to be accountable
Know how to apologize
Know how to forgive yourself
Know how to "clean yourself up"

Humbleness is key
Egos take leave
Remember this in all you do

No matter how far you go
No matter what you become
No matter what you believe

This life is truly so much about mindset

Oppressions will occur in this life
And how to deal with them
Is different for each person
I can't guarantee
That you will deal with oppressions, correctly
But I will say
That you have the theory on how to deal
Now you have to put the theory into action

When you're down
The people in your corner
Will know how to empathize
And not sympathize
When need be

See,
A sympathetic person will always
Go on a tangent
By saying some form of the following phrase
"At least you…"
That's not always what you need…

Realize that certain situations
Call for no words
They only call for action…
And that action
May only be a tight hug or long cuddle

As you grow,
You'll find those people who do this innately
Without you ever saying anything
Remember,
Genuine love showcases actions naturally
Even if…
In spite of…
And no matter if…

When you're up,
The people in your corner
Will celebrate you
Or with you,
Like it was their personal win

Figure out what's fun for you

And make that a source of income
And what you're passionate about
Make that your career

Yes, life calls for many sacrifices
But ultimately
If you can live off your passion
And your idea of fun
Then life will be all-the-more spectacular

Be unconventional
Think about new ways to tackle problems
Problem solvers will be abundantly needed
In the society of tomorrow

For finance and real estate
Even if it's not your career field...
Learn about trusts
Learn about buying, selling, trading
Learn about land-use
Learn about zoning
Learn about taxes
Learn how having a business
Even if it churns no money
Can be a tax break if you primarily have earned income from a 9-5
Learn about foreign accounts
Understand from a code-level
Line-by-line
What the the blockchain is
Learn about 529 accounts
Learn about 1031 exchanges
Learn the rigorous mathematic and statistical techniques
On how an economy works

For technology
Learn how to be in-the-know
Learn how to implement, simulate, and preach
From a 100-level to a 500-level

For skills
Learn what's fun for you
Learn how to turn raw materials
Into vacuum chambers or natural antibiotics
If that's fun for you...

Learn the essential aspects associated with architecture
Or welding
Or off-roading
Or piloting
Or hair styling
Or making videos
Or art
Or bread making
Or whatever the case may be for you

For your development
Learn how to believe and trust in something
Greater than yourself
Learn religious texts
Learn about history

Be aware of bad things that aren't for you
And silence them throughout your life

But you see,
I could give the knowledge behind my interests
And how I did or do certain things
But I must say...

Learning all of this doesn't equate to too much
If never put into action
And experienced for yourself

So that leads to...
Be okay with not having all the answers
You have to figure out
How to maneuver the jungle for yourself

You must be confident in yourself
And what you bring to the table
Man or woman...
Some folks can get a sense of who they are dealing with
Once that person walks into the room

Know how to read a room
Know when to be quiet
Know when to speak

Smile often

Laugh uncontrollably sometimes
Take a chance
Take a risk

Discover those experiences
Landscapes
And places
That most will never see

And realize that,
Conviction
Morals
Respect
Integrity
And intelligence

Are and always will be
In style

Embrace who you are
From me to you,

You gotta be…you

27. THE DAWN OF A SUNSET

I found myself harping on the art of letting go, lately
It's quite a pesky thing to do
And truly an art
When needed to be done...
But for good people it can be challenging

I'm a firm believer in the fact that
When you find someone
You not only marry them
But if they have a close or loving family
You're also marrying yourself into that as well
I feel like people forget about that fact nowadays

So many things to ponder on...
Let me get right into it

The four fundamental forces of nature are
Electromagnetic
Gravity
Strong
And weak

But I'm a meshfree method
What do I mean?
I mean that:
I can freely move
I can deform
I can tangle
I can obstruct

Thus, I'm not precise
And definitively bound
I'm truly not a standardized individual
Who can be categorized
By unexplored means
I am rogue
At times, more than others

I'm human
I struggle
I have beliefs

And I have things about me
That others don't like...
And I'm cool with that

I'm full of layers
I observe intently...
When genuinely called upon
I tell myself to fully engage and give my all

I am a system of sorts
A miraculous system

It's really insane to think about what we can do
As humans, we've been granted so much
And we can even create things better than us

I enjoy running
The freedom I feel
When embedded in nature
To chart unknown landscapes to me
Is exhilarating in all regards

A beautiful, boundless world
With laws awaiting to be discovered
Or maybe its "laws" aren't always definitive either

The only thing on this Earth
That seems to really drive the people
That occupy it
Is currency

You know...
Hearing that doesn't have the same effect
On me as it once did
There's so much more out there

There's so much goodness
There's so much love
There's so much appreciation
There's so much trust

But 'tis the world we live
And I will contribute my justification
To society as well

I was reading a story today
About a person who had it all financially
Worked their butt off, tirelessly
And then they were diagnosed,
Quite early in their life,
With transient onset amnesia
And after reading the story
All I could think was,
"Was it all worth it?
Did you make the genuine impact before the tragedy?"

I've blabbered this whole journal entry
Let me pinpoint my direction…

I've grown a great deal
I feel like I'm sincerely older than my birth age
I want this next chapter,
Chapter 1 of my life,
To be filled with goodness
With the things I have control over
I want to say goodbye to the me
Who had badness about him

I've surrendered and came back stronger
I study intensely, every week
Because the dawn of my chapter 1
Is coming

And I'm ready
My friends
They're ready too
Ready for what we'll face in this lifetime
Ready for failing more than succeeding
Ready for learning
Ready to have fun
Ready to showcase the goodness
Ready to tell the good news
For…

The sunset reaches
With its claws
For the atmosphere that needs it most
Dazzling

Spawning brightly with its color
It's a phenomenon that heals
Surely mesmerizing
And perplexing the nouns
Of uninhabited and habited space
It's defined…
Defined by the principles of science
Regulated by the conclusions of the atmosphere
Discussed by the habited nomenclature…
It's relied upon
In the cycle of things that make the world
Magnificent…
The organisms that are in its clutches
Are not so well-defined
Yes, many are the same with a different face
In the literal and figurative sense
But there are abnormalities…
What if the sunset, every now and again, performed dire, odd behavior?
Of which was beyond reason, rules, or principles
That's what makes me feel so relieved
To know that there's a new leaf, we can turn
With relative ease…
We don't have to remain the same
Nor do we have to point a finger
And blame
We are humanity

We are
We can
We try
We will

Believe

A LAST WORD…

THE STRUCTURE IN THE CLOUDS

There was a pink sky
I was cruising
Only for the picturesque visuals
And miscellaneous thoughts...
No cars in sight
Nor was I feeling uptight
I felt relieved
Commonalities to cryogenic slumber
On how my soul felt...
I felt so free

I arrived at my destination
I was in a spectacular awe
I felt the vibes of a summer night
A sky that made my eyes light
And a landscape visual that could only be molded by Father Time

"They won't have history like we do..."
Is what I thought to myself
What I meant was...
The vast majority of people
Would never know of this amazing spectacle
And that could also be what's made it so special
It invoked me to take action...

I walked down from the cliff
I was alone,
But the I wore the souls
Around my neck
Of those who are in my heart abreast
So they were with me

I then came to the stream...

Standing firm
I asked God to grant me victory,
Grant me understanding
Grant me valor
For I wanted to start anew
Cause I have so much to do

"I can't let the burdens of the past overtake me,"
I pleaded
"For I am a man who is all about knowledge
Thus,
I'd never be able to move forward properly
With anchors on my feet"

God
A Creator
Or something spiritual
Spoke to me that day
Through somebody
Cause as I waited for feedback
Absorbing the environment around me,
I got a random call

The person described everything I needed to hear
And more
Without me saying or doing anything
I knew again that God had not forsaken me

I went back up the cliff
Got back in the vehicle
So I could travel on the gnarly terrain
That made this picturesque visual so insane…

Only thought to myself was
"We must protect this"
We've been granted a resilient planet
We must take the steps
To ensure our longevity
And ensure the longevity
Of our surroundings

I've now gotten more ideas to venture on…

As I get closer to seeing my one dream
Come to fruition
I'm always reminded that,
We are one species

Until the next time
Where I will discuss chapter 1 of my life…

Please take care
~Cam

CAMERON MCKNIGHT

Made in the USA
Columbia, SC
06 May 2022

60033304R00046